Discover the secret to personal fulfillment and lasting success. Learn how to harness the power of your imagination, creativity, and inner potential to change your attitudes and realize your dreams. The *Mind Magic Kit* is your key to the life you've always wished you could have.

The *Mind Magic Kit* demonstrates how you can cultivate relaxing, rejuvenating, and life-enhancing states of mind that will eliminate mental tension and stress instantly. Achieve optimum performance, increased health, and stimulate your body's natural ability to reverse aging, fight cancer, and improve your general state of fitness and well-being.

*"I've learned more from this one person than I have from anyone else through his powerful, effective, and efficiently condensed experiential instruction."*

Carl Llewellyn Weschcke
President, Llewellyn Worldwide

## About the Author

Dr. Jonn Mumford, DO, DC (Swami Anandakapila Saraswati), is a direct disciple of Dr. Swami Gitananda (South India) and Paramahansa Swami Satyananda Saraswati, Bihar, by whom he was initiated in 1973. Dr. Mumford is respected across the world for his knowledge and scholarship. He frequently lectures on relaxation techniques, sexuality, Tantra, and other aspects of human development and spirituality.

Dr. Mumford is a world-renowned authority on Tantra and yoga. He has demonstrated his own self-mastery of cardiac cessation, obliteration of individual pulse beat at will, sensory withdrawal and voluntary breath retention over the five-minute range, and start and stop bleeding on command.

His background combining years of experience as a physician with extensive international experience in a wide range of Eastern disciplines makes Dr. Jonn Mumford eminently well suited to the task of disseminating the secrets of Tantra to the West. He currently divides his time between South India, the United States, and Australia.

Internet Contact: "Dr. Jonn Mumford's Home Page" at http://www.ozemail.com.au/~mumford8.

## To Write to the Author

If you wish to contact the author or would like more information about this book, please write to the author in care of Llewellyn Worldwide, and we will forward your request. Both the author and publisher appreciate hearing from you. Llewellyn Worldwide cannot guarantee that every letter written to the author can be answered, but all will be forwarded. Please write to:

*Llewellyn's New Worlds of Mind and Spirit*
P.O. Box 64383, Dept. K475–8,
St. Paul, MN 55164-0383, U.S.A.

Please enclose a self-addressed, stamped envelope for reply, or $1.00 to cover costs. If outside the U.S.A., enclose international postal reply coupon

# MIND MAGIC KIT

## Dr. Jonn Mumford, DO, DC
### (Swami Anandakapila Saraswati)

1998
Llewellyn Publications
St. Paul, Minnesota, U.S.A. 55164-0383

FIRST EDITION
First Printing, 1998

Cover design by Tom Grewe
Cover photo by Digital Stock © 1997
Editing and interior design by Connie Hill


Library of Congress Cataloging-in-Publication Data
Mumford, Jonn
    Mind magic kit / Jonn Mumford. — 1st ed.
        p.    cm.  — )
        Includes bibliographical references and index.
        ISBN 1-56718-475–8  (pbk.)
    1. Relaxation.   2. Stress management.    3. Mind and
body.   I. Title.
RA785.M85    1998
613.7'9—dc21                                        97-44746
                                                        CIP



Llewellyn Publications
A Division of Llewellyn Worldwide, Ltd.
St. Paul, Minnesota 55164-0383, U.S.A.

Printed in the U.S.A.

## Dedication

To Paramahamsa Niranjanananda Saraswati,
the Acharya of the Bihar School of Yoga,
Sivananda Math, Yoga Research Foundation
and the Bihar Yoga Bharati (Yoga
University), Bihar State, India.
His life is an inspiration to thousands
of yoga students and disciples.

## Other Books by the Author

*Psychosomatic Yoga*
*Ecstasy Through Tantra*
*A Chakra & Kundalini Workbook*
*Magical Tattwas*

## Forthcoming

*Death: Beginning or End?*
*How to Clear Your Karma in 9 Days*

# Table of Contents

# Acknowledgments

I would like to thank Cheryl Stevens who assembled my material for the *Mind Magic Kit*, organized it on the computer, supported me, and patiently taught me the fundamentals of computing to prepare for the twenty-first century.

# 1
# What Is Mind Magic?

● ━━━━━━━━━

## A CRAM Course

Mind Magic is **stress reduction** for the twenty-first century—**now**!

It is my pleasure to introduce you to a mental reconditioning technique that I have spent over a decade evolving. The *Mind Magic Kit* is the result of successfully merging elements of both Eastern and Western psychology. In a sense, we could call this program you now possess a **CRAM** course, in the literal sense of the word.

**CRAM** is the facilitation of **C**oncentration, **R**elaxation, **A**ttitudinal change, and **M**editation.

You will achieve **CRAM** by using this program—and **CRAM** means just that! You are going to improve your *concentration* skills, your *relaxation* response, your ability to change your *attitudes*, and your general *meditative* skills.

I am proud of the Mind Magic program because, through experience with thousands of people, I have proved it works!

Those who attend my Mind Magic workshops attest to its effectiveness.

> I used to feel the blood rising in my face and think I was about to burst with anger; now I concentrate on sending the blood to my hands instead.
>
> Geoff
> Payroll Officer

Suzanne, a management consultant, comments, "Instead of being hassled when things go wrong, I show the people around me that I can make one of my hands warm and the other cold instead of getting upset."

Mind Magic brings together the best of East and West for the purpose of achieving Relaxation, Self-Hypnosis, and Meditation—FAST!

## A De-Stressing Program

**Mind Magic** is a dynamic program that I have developed to provide you with the keys to unwinding stress, controlling circulation, and learning autogenic temperature control techniques.

You will master migraine, anxiety, tension headaches, Raynaud's disease, nervousness, panic attacks, and insomnia.

Recently the Journal *Headache* published an Australian research project demonstrating a sixty-eight percent improvement in tension and migraine headaches in a group of pregnant women using only **Fractional Relaxation** (Progressive Relaxation) and **Thermal Biofeedback.** That abstract was produced in May 1996 and by the end of the Mind Magic program, Fractional Relaxation and Thermal Biofeedback will become very familiar to you.

Controlling high blood pressure is possibly the best-researched advantage of educing the **Relaxation Response** (see Dr. Herbert Benson's book of the same title[1]).

## Stimulating the Rejuvenation Hormone

Not only will this program alleviate psychosomatic illnesses, but evidence is accumulating that relaxation, meditation, and stress reduction

---

1  Herbert Benson and Miriam Z. Klipper, *Relaxation Response* (Avon, 1976).

routines increase secretion of the pineal hormone **Melatonin** with consequent implications for rejuvenation, retarding aging, and anti-carcinogenic benefits!

Melatonin is a substance secreted from the pineal gland and it represents possibly the most important hormone investigated in the last fifteen years. Until about twenty years ago the pineal gland was dismissed as a "vestigial" or useless, redundant organ in the middle of the brain—this in spite of two facts!

- An ancient Indian Yoga tradition had always equated the pineal gland with the "Third Eye"—a psychic center in the forehead called "Ajna Chakra."

- Physiologists had recognized that the pineal gland had the second largest blood supply in the body, after the kidneys; given this knowledge, construing the pineal gland as "a useless leftover" is a sad commentary on how short-sighted Western medical science can sometimes be!

Melatonin, released by your pineal gland, has been discovered to have a multitude of beneficial effects and not only is it now widely taken as a prophylactic against jet lag but it is indicated as:

- As an anti-aging treatment; peak levels of Melatonin have dropped by half in people over sixty, compared with twenty-year-olds. Research scientists at McGill University in Montreal and the University of Texas Health Science Center in San Antonio, Texas, are working on this factor.

- Melatonin is the "mother" of all **antioxidants.** Since the early 1990s information has been accumulating that Melatonin is stronger than either vitamin C or vitamin E in preventing the profusion of "free-radicals" (free-radicals encourage degenerative disease).

- Melatonin strongly inhibits the growth of many types of cancer cells.

In the United States, the University of Massachusetts Medical Center recorded a higher level of melatonin in students meditating as part of the university's stress reduction and relaxation program (reported in *Brain/Mind*, June 1996).

As a key speaker at the Sydney, Australia, World Yoga Convention in October 1996 (sponsored by the Saraswati Order under the auspices of Paramahamsa Niranjanananda), I was privileged to hear Greg Tooley (a doctoral candidate at

Deakin University, School of Psychology) give the results of his research working with La Trobe University, the University of Melbourne, and the Anti-Cancer Council of Victoria. He has independently demonstrated increased levels of Melatonin in meditators in a study yet to be released in the United States.

This study demonstrated that melatonin may be a specific physiological marker for meditation. melatonin thus explains the subjective extra benefits reported by Meditators. Greg did a study with the well-known T.M. (Transcendental Meditation) group and another Yoga group of meditators who utilized a totally different technique. The results were exactly the same in both groups—that meditation increases melatonin in the body, with all its attendant advantages.

## Melatonin and Yoga: The Adelaide University Research Project

Even more exciting is the research being conducted by a Swami of the Saraswati order at Adelaide University, South Australia. In the words of Swami Sannyasananda:

"Greg Tooley's work involved looking at melatonin levels around midnight, whereas my research is looking at melatonin levels around the time of onset of melatonin, which differs for each person, but occurs some time between sunset and the individual's normal bedtime. By exploring the effects of different neural inputs using certain Tantric yoga practices, we can tease out how the brain is wired up and functions as a whole. To be able to do this work, a system with a stable common marker or neurological flag is used to see what happens to that marker when we manipulate internal states. The marker for my research is the hormone Melatonin.

> Melatonin is a potent oncostatic agent; it prevents both the initiation and promotion of cancer and therefore plays an important role in the immune system.
>
> Swami Sannyasananda

"Melatonin is a pineal hormone implicated in the control of a wide array of behavioral and physiological rhythms that include movement, sleep cycles, body temperature regulation, cardiovascular function, stress responses, the female estrous cycle and many other endocrine processes. Melatonin is also a useful marker in examining many disorders of rhythms and is an extremely important substance for a number of reasons.

"It is the pineal gland, a small pea-sized organ deep within the brain, that produces most of the melatonin in our bodies, though small amounts are produced in the eyes and also in the gut. Normally the pineal produces low levels of melatonin during the day and high amounts at night. Exposure to light at night is followed by a drop in melatonin levels, since the eyes are functionally connected to the pineal gland by a series of neurons.

"Reduction of melatonin, at night, by any means, increases cells' vulnerability to carcinogenic agents. An increased cancer incidence has also been reported in environments exposed to higher than normal artificial electromagnetic fields that lead to a reduction in nighttime levels of melatonin. Melatonin is a potent oncostatic agent; it prevents both the initiation and promotion of cancer and therefore plays an important role in the immune system. It is a potent antioxidant and may provide significant protection against cancer. Melatonin induces activated T cells to release opioid peptides with immune enhancing and anti-stress properties. These peptides cross-react and bind specifically to thymus receptors, driving an immune recovery after elevated corticosteroid levels associated with immune responses and/or stressful situations.

"Because of the powerful effects of melatonin, there are many research programs, often using animals, to model various effects. Human physiology is different to animals, though, and as such some of this research is of little use or relevance to humans. The practice of yoga does not require animal experiments and makes use of live human volunteers yielding valuable information. There are two main areas of interest for me regarding melatonin research and the psychoneurophysiology of certain Tantric yoga practices. One of the practices of Nadi Shodhan is *Pranayama* (alternate nostril breathing), and the other is the practice of *Tratak* (focusing the eyes by staring at a candle flame, Yantra or dot). Both of these practices affect the brain in profound ways."[2]

Swami Sannyasananda is currently completing research projects on the neurological effects of these Tantric practices at Adelaide University Medical School. You can read the full abstract in

---

2 Printed with permission of Swami Sannyasananda.

appendix 2, and I will tell you that ten minutes of quiet gazing at a candle flame before bedtime, coupled with the secret Bija Mantra I will teach you, opens the floodgates of what I call the "Magic Melatonin Meditation." I will reveal this in chapter 10.

Mind Magic opens the gates of meditation.

I will teach you a **secret key code word**, that as part of the **autogenic training,** will move you into deep **meditation** states, with all the attendant advantages, including increased Melatonin secretions.

You will complete this program knowing exactly **how, why,** and **when** to apply the **autogenic temperature control techniques** and you will have the tools to retain the skills!

These autogenic temperature control techniques involve using the thermometer and cassette tape provided in this kit to provide you with the temperature control feedback you need to reduce and eventually eliminate stress.

# 2

# Modifying Attitudes and Self-Image with Mind Magic

●━━━━━━━━━

## The Power of Attitude

What we are dealing with in the Mind Magic program is a combination of East and West, Indian yoga and European medical techniques that have the potential to change our attitudes and modify our reactivity to stressful events.

Our attitudes are frequently determined by the very words we use in our head.

If we change the words that go around in our heads we begin to change our feel-

> Men are disturbed not by things, but by the views which they take of them.
>
> Epictetus
> 2nd Century A.D.

ings and the way we react to life. It is a question in life of attitudes versus facts and very frequently we find that the attitudes we possess are more important than the facts.

## Fact and Fallacy

American psychologist Dr. Albert Ellis founded an influential school of psychotherapy called "Cognitive Therapy" or "Rational Emotive Therapy."

The basis of Ellis' system is focused on the fallacies or false ideas concerning ourselves, and unreasonable expectations about life. These "fallacies," false premises, or illogical concepts can wreak emotional havoc in our lives if not questioned. (See appendix 3 for exercises dealing with fallacies.)

In his excellent book *A New Guide to Rational Living,* Ellis examines a number of these irrational "fallacies." He states that if something is dangerous or potentially dangerous, we become preoccupied with the possibility of its occurring.[1]

A major key to philosophical living is dwelling in the present. Consider the following statement from Dr. Jim Dreaver's excellent book, *The Ultimate Cure* (Llewellyn Publications, 1995):

---

1  Albert Ellis and Robert A. Harper, *A New Guide to Rational Living* (Wilshire).

"As you master the art of living in the present—of 'present-time consciousness,' as some call it—the past and the future come into their right perspective. Everything you've learned in the past, all the knowledge you've acquired, is available to you should you need it, but you are not psychologically or emotionally bound by it. Similarly, you can visualize and make such plans for the future as are necessary or appropriate, but you're no longer seduced by false hopes, idle daydreams, or wishful thinking. Once you know your destination, your goal, you can let it go—put it at the back of your mind, so to speak—and relish the journey."[2]

There is a distinct line drawn between awareness of possible danger in certain situations versus a fearful concern of **phobic proportions** in which the mind is living in **imaginary anticipation** of future calamity.

When we become anxious over an imagined future tragedy, we are really reacting to the fantasy of an event that has just occurred **only** in our **mind,** but we are responding as if it had occurred in **reality**!

---

2  Jim Dreaver, *The Ultimate Cure* (St. Paul: Llewellyn Publications, 1996).

I can express this more aptly by saying our nervous system is aroused by mental events as surely as by physical contingencies. The human nervous system does not know the difference between fantasy and reality!

## Over 1,500 Years of Understanding

This is by no means a modern idea or a contemporary discovery, as St. Augustine wrote in his *Confessions* (fifth century A.D.): "Why is it that man desires to be made sad, beholding doleful and tragical things, which yet himself by no means would suffer?"

> People can die of mere imagination.
>
> Geoffrey Chaucer
> *The Canterbury Tales*
> (c. 1387–1400)

## Attitude versus Fact

There is a difference between attitude and fact, and attitudes are everything!

The theologian Frederick Langrebridge, in the 1870s, expressed basically the same concept when he said "two men look out through the bars, one sees the mud and one the stars," and that pretty well sums up the human situation. The question has also been asked, "Are we in a prison—or is the prison in us?"

> Stone walls do not a prison make, Nor iron bars a cage, Minds innocent and quiet take that for a hermitage.
>
> Richard Lovelace (1618–1658)

The Mind Magic program produces a **quiet mind** and restores **innocence**! Remove the stress from the mind and that which appears to entrap us gently dissolves, allowing childlike innocence to return to a simpler and happier person.

## How Does the Mind Magic Program Work for You?

Initially the Mind Magic program focuses on gaining temperature control in one hand, which quickly expands to both hands and then to other parts of the body. This control, combined with the physical relaxation techniques (Side One; Fractional Relaxation), naturally and

> A man who fears suffering is already suffering from what he fears.
>
> Michel De Montaigne *Essays* (1533–1592)

easily prepares you to **rapidly** drop into **deep meditation states.**

The accompanying quotation takes us into the seventeenth century with a perfect description of what would now be termed "pilomotor nerve activation due to sudden arousal of fear, fight, flight state" (hair standing on end and goose-bumps) with accompanying "psychogenic tachycardia" (anxiety-induced racing heart):

Whose horrid image doth unfix my hair
and make my seated heart knock at my ribs,
against the use of nature? Present fears
are less than horrible imaginings.

Shakespeare
*Macbeth* 1: 111
(c. 1610)

# 3

# What Is the Mind Magic Program?

●━━━━━━━━

## Mind Magic Kit

In the kit you receive this book, an audio tape with **"Fractional Relaxation"** on one side and **"Autogenic Temperature Training"** on the other, and a **Biofeedback Thermometer.**

These tools provide you with everything you need to **CRAM.**

Remember: **CRAM** is an acronym that sums up the benefits of this training method—a vastly improved ability for Concentration, Relaxation, Attitudinal Change and Meditation.

**When you complete this program
the methods are literally
IN YOUR HANDS!**

All of the techniques in this program are easily mastered with a minimum of practice. Fractional relaxation and autogenic temperature training are skills that can be mastered by anyone. **Daily use** of either side one or side two for at least several months will establish **balance and integration** within your nervous system, resulting in a new level of "calm" being experienced.

## What Is Fractional Relaxation?

Fractional Relaxation deals with physical tension first, followed by eliminating mental tension and cultivating life-affirming states of mind.

Frederick Mathias Alexander (1869–1955), the founder of the "Alexander School" of posture and movement, expressed the situation very well: "You translate everything, whether physical or mental or spiritual, into muscular tension."[1]

Relaxing unnecessarily contracted muscles is not losing control—it is gaining control! Physical relaxation not only conserves energy but for most of us is a precursor to mental relaxation.

The physical relaxation techniques divide into two parts: first what we might term *tension,*

---

1   F. Matthias Alexander, *The Resurrection of the Body,* edited by Edward Maisel (New York: Dell Publishing. 1969).

followed by *relaxation*. This is also called "Progressive Relaxation." Fractional relaxation is the progressive contraction and release of the voluntary muscles in the body.

On the first side of the accompanying audiotape you will be asked to tense certain major muscle groups and then relax them, principally the limbs. After that, we will begin a systematic process of fractional relaxation in which I will speak to you, encouraging you to let go and feel heavy. In my school we always work from the head, the center of consciousness, down to the feet, so that we are relaxing more and more deeply.

> The greatest knowledge is power over the self.
>
> Dr. Jonn Mumford

## What Is Autogenic Temperature Training?

"Autogenic" means "self-generated." On the second side of the accompanying audiotape I will teach you a proven method to increase the temperature in your hands and feet and enjoy a deep meditative state that can be recalled, with practice, by using the simple code word "**CALM**."

The other tool in this *Mind Magic Kit* is a biofeedback thermometer (shown below). Autogenic temperature control using a biofeedback thermometer is your personal proof of **mind over matter**!

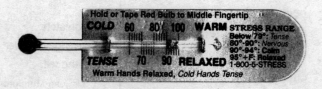

The simple truth is …
>  Cold hands = tension
>  Warm hands = relaxation

Most of us are "hand reactors"—that is, we respond to anxiety and tension states by automatically contracting the arterioles feeding blood into the hands, thus reducing the temperature in the hands (blood carries heat!).

## Experiment

The next time you feel tense, apprehensive, or anxious, place your dominant hand on the back of your neck. Your hand will probably feel cold against the back of your neck. The temperature of the tissue in the back of the neck never varies while the hand temperature tends to fluctuate, according to mood (hence "mood rings") from 60° Fahrenheit to 95° Fahrenheit.

**You will learn not to be a reactive human "barometer" and how to take control!**

# 4

# What Is Deep Relaxation?

## Hypnosis versus Deep Relaxation

For many people, there is a rather blurred relationship between the concepts of hypnosis and deep relaxation. The two states are often not clearly differentiated from each other.

Indeed, for many, the word "hypnosis" is a scare word. Hypnosis and relaxation-meditation are not the same thing—however, they share a common factor. This factor we would call *monoideism* in the West or *ekagrata* (that's Sanskrit for "one pointedness" or "single pointedness"). Both terms mean focused attention. This single pointedness of attention that manifests in hypnosis also manifests in the inducing of the relaxation response and is a natural psychophysical state.

Daydreaming while *performing simple tasks and not remembering that you did them* is an example of the "relaxation-trance" state that everyone has experienced. So hypnosis, relaxation, and meditation are not exactly the same things, but they share this common feature of focusing the mind.

It is an interesting discovery of Western psychology that people who are so-called "good hypnotic subjects" do not necessarily find it easier to meditate. On the other hand, constant practice of meditation does greatly facilitate the ability to benefit from suggestion.

## Suggestibility

As you learn to relax with me on the first side of the accompanying audiotape, I don't want you to be concerned with concepts of hypnosis, but rather be concerned with the fact that through deep relaxation you can place yourself into a non-critical mental state in which you can change your self-concept and your self-image.

Let me offer a rough differentiation between hypnosis and meditation. Let us say that what is popularly called hypnosis is a state of hyper-suggestibility, **a non-critical state in which you will accept suggestions,** provided they are not injurious (mentally or physically) to your well-being. You will accept positive suggestions encouraging an altered self-image and altered attitudes about yourself.

Conversely, we could say that one aspect of meditation is that it is **a non-critical mental state** in which you accept totally yourself, your being-ness, and your relationship to the entire life process of existence.

## Control by Self or Another

When we begin to relax, when we begin to experience hypnosis, or meditation states, there are a number of common misconceptions. The very first point I would like to make is that it is impossible for someone else to hypnotize you or place you in a meditative state. Notwithstanding this, by common agreement between us you may use my words on the accompanying audiotape to facilitate your relaxation.

It is a basic dictum that no one else can alter your state of consciousness without your consent and cooperation (barring severe brain-washing methods). Briefly, all hypnosis is self-hypnosis, as is relaxation and meditation. We begin these states and end them for ourselves—and of course when we begin to relax, when we begin to meditate, we have certain primitive fears.

## Losing Control

One very common fear that is expressed when people discuss hypnosis is that a relaxed, hypnotized, or meditating person will become unconscious. This question arises because many of us have a normal fear or dislike of losing consciousness, that is losing control, in spite of the fact that we do so every night by *falling asleep*.

I will repeat this several times. Relaxing, experiencing hypnotic states, and meditating are not situations in which you **lose control**—on the contrary, they are circumstances in which you are **in control**—being tense and anxious is "*losing control*!"

The fact is that in these altered states of consciousness we are always completely aware of what is happening or know what we are saying or doing. We do not lose consciousness in the true sense that we become unconscious or comatose, that is, incapable of being brought out of the hypnotic state or of bringing ourselves out of the state.

It is very unfortunate that this word "hypnosis" comes from the Greek word for "sleep," and thus has facilitated exactly this kind of confusion. Equally silly is the idea that somebody else controls the depths of relaxation that we experience. In fact, the subject, the participant, the person who goes into a relaxed state at all times controls the depth. It is we, ourselves, that prevent the induction of our relaxation or hold ourselves back from reaching deeper states. No one does anything in relaxation or goes any deeper than they are ready for at that given moment.

## Coming Out

Another common fear when we relax, meditate or enjoy unusual experiences of the mind is that we may not wake up. When we were talking about straight clinical hypnosis, the question arises if you believe the fallacy that somebody hypnotizes you (in fact only you are capable of hypnotizing yourself—all hypnosis is self-hypnosis) then what is going to happen if your hypnotist has a coronary? Are you going to stay in that trance state?

**Of course not!**

When we are deeply relaxed, when we meditate, or when we are in what is loosely called "a state of hypnosis," if we are left alone we will come out of it as naturally as we awaken from ordinary sleep when we have had enough.

There are cases, of course, where people go into special trance states and they appear not to want to come out.

Sometimes people appear to have difficulty in awakening, displaying great reluctance to relinquish the pleasurable state they are experiencing. This has to do with motive.

Naturally if you are enjoying an extremely comfortable state of mind and if you are temporarily free from an unpleasant environment, you may dislike having to come back to waking consciousness.

# 5

# Preparation for Relaxation

●━━━━━━━━━━

## State of Mind

There are several preliminary rules I'd like to discuss with you before you embark on your actual inner life experience, your inner space journey of fractional relaxation, or as we call it in India: *Shavasana*.

### Anxiety Blocks Relaxation

The first major thing to understand is that we should never attempt a relaxation procedure or a mind-altering state when we are **acutely anxious**, as this will block relaxation.

You know that when an express train first begins to move off from the station, throwing a brick on the track will stop it instantly, but once the express train is going 100 miles an hour, there is no way to stop it.

And so it is that if we become acutely anxious (that means we are shaking, we feel nauseated, we are white in the face), then attempting to relax or meditate while in such a state is like attempting to stop the express train once it is going 100 miles an hour.

We have to run around the block, go for a swim, talk the problem over with a friend, have a hot bath, or find some way to bring our nervous system out of the acute sympathetic arousal of fear-fight-flight reactions.

## Techniques to Reduce Anxiety

A very effective method for dealing with acute anxiety before relaxing is ten to fifteen minutes of careful rhythmic breathing exercises.

These need not be advanced or complicated and, for those who are not sophisticated in their yoga technique, there is a very simple rule. **Breathe as slowly as possible,** so slowly that you are not able to hear your own incoming breath. Accompany this breathing with the following very simple visualization exercise.

As you breathe in, imagine that you see a feather hanging by a thread from the ceiling, about an inch from your nose. Now, breathe out so slowly that in your imagination the feather does not move or tremble.

Alternately, you can visualize a candle flame magically suspended in space, perhaps two inches from your nose. You are breathing so slowly, so fully, breathing out so carefully, that the candle flame does not bend or flicker.

# Environment

## Place

The fractional relaxation technique on the first side of the accompanying audiotape is best done lying down—either on a bed or on a carpeted floor.

## Warmth

Preparation for deep relaxation involves common sense. Naturally, if we are to relax, we need a warm, comfortable environment.

Use a blanket to provide the comfort reminiscent of sleep. A cover over yourself is also important because we tend to lose body heat when deeply relaxed or in a hypnotic state. This is due to increased circulation just under the skin; the blood radiates heat from the body.

## Comfort

Do not hesitate to use pillows, if necessary, under the knees—this is very important if you suffer low back pain. A small pillow behind the back of the head may also help to make some people more comfortable.

## Quiet

Taking the phone off the hook or turning on the answering machine is also essential, as well as selecting a time that guarantees you will not be disturbed by others.

## Time for Ourselves

The goal of preparation is to arrange a set of circumstances that permit us to create time for ourselves—in the twentieth century we desperately need time to reintegrate the "self" and recoup our life energies.

Mind Magic practices are specifically designed to provide deep refreshment each day, thus enabling us

> Resolute imagination is the beginning of all magical operations.
>
> Paracelsus

to function with much more ease and efficiency. It is truly amazing for some of us to realize how conditioned we are to feeling guilty about taking time out to restore our own inner energies.

# Body Positioning

## Face Up — Natural Fetal Position

The preferred position is for you to lie down, face up, in what we call the anatomical position, the Shavasana Position, which is really the natural fetal position but you've simply unflexed. The palms of the hands are about twelve inches from the body and turned upwards (the palms are always turned upward, if possible).

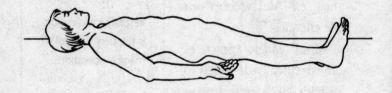

## Palms Up

I prefer that people do not attempt to relax with their palms down. There are physiological reasons for this. You know that the touch receptors on the fingertips are so sensitive that the blind learn to read Braille through their fingertips. If your hands are palms down, there is a certain subtle stimulation of tactile receptors which tends to maintain a response in the brain through the reticular system.

By turning the hands palm up, we avoid this stimulation; as well as the physiological reason, there is an actual anatomical reason.

## Arms at Side

If you've done a first aid course, and you know what an anatomical position is (a person standing

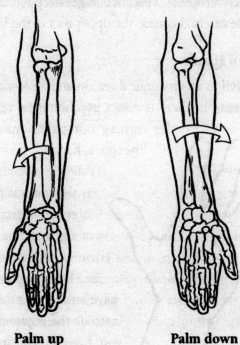

**Palm up**                    **Palm down**

upright with the hands hanging by the sides, palms facing forward) then you will realize that this is a special position in which the two bones of the lower arm—the radius bone (on the thumb side) and the ulnar bone (on the little finger side)—lie side by side.

These two bones in the lower arm, lying neatly side by side, prevent a membrane that connects them (interosseous membrane) from firing little stretch receptors. This encourages deep relaxation of the cerebral cortex, the upper part of the brain.

## Open Hands

As well as an anatomical reason and a physiological reason, there is also a psychological reason for turning our palms upward: the open-handed position, called *shunya mudra*, is the natural position of surrender, of giving in, of trust, of confidence.

You know if you and I have an argument and I concede the argument to you, I give in, I shrug my shoulders, and I open my hands—empty and in the surrender position. Indeed, the handshake originated to show that the hand was empty— that there was no malicious intent. When we turn our palms up, we are always symbolizing trust, surrender, and receptivity to the deep unconscious levels of our being.

### If You Cannot Physically Place Your Hands "Palm Up"!

Fractures, dislocation, strains, sprains, and various types of arthritis may make it impossible to comfortably rest your hands palm up.

The next optimum position (for reducing tactile alerting responses to the brain) is resting the hands on the little finger edge. The fists may be semi-closed, with the thumbnails pointing upward at the ceiling, as shown here.

### Feet Apart and Falling Outward (Eversion)

Another major preparation factor is that your feet are to be at least twelve inches apart and turned outward.

Some yoga schools teach you to do relaxation with the heels together. As far as we are concerned, this is incorrect. It actually increases tension in the muscles of the thigh, the groin, the perineum, and the urogenital area. We want the feet a minimum of twelve inches apart so that the feet naturally evert or turn outward. In so doing the muscles on the inside of your thighs (related to the urogenital complex) are released and relaxed. The legs are relaxed and eased completely and totally as you sink deeper and deeper into the "relaxation response" experience.

## Avoiding Muscle Cramps

A word about "contraction-release" techniques on side one (Fractional Relaxation) of the *Mind Magic* Audio Cassette

**Do not over-contract!** Adjust the contraction of muscle groups in your body to your own individual level. Always avoid cramping or strain.

Some of us are particularly susceptible to cramping of the small muscles of the foot and the calf muscle. If you have a tendency to cramp in the calf muscle do not contract the muscles of the leg by "pointing the toes" or making a "ballet point" (as my voice will instruct you). Instead pull your toes and foot back toward the kneecap (dorsiflexing rather than plantar flexing). Think of this as "bowing" the foot to the knee.

My friend, Paul Solomon, was the person I learned this refinement from. Avoid cramping at all costs! It plays havoc with a relaxation session!

## If Doing Physical Contractions Is Not Useful!

Some people find that the contraction and release techniques in the first part of the fractional relaxation are more of a hindrance than a help. What to do?

Use the Mumford "SSS" rule! Instead of contracting the body part, e.g., limb:

1. **Sense** the body part—feel it—be aware of sensations from it.

2. **See** it—visualize or imagine it.

3. **Say** it—mentally repeat the instruction on the tape (this is the echo).

Realize that imagining you have contracted a body part will produce micro-contractions through a mind-body arc. No thought or image passes through the mind without a corresponding physical reaction.

# 6

# Techniques to Improve Your Relaxation

●━━━━━━━━━━

## Echo Technique

### "My thoughts won't stop!"

We are now ready to deal with the solution to a problem that every teacher and every yoga student encounters. How often do we hear students say that they are able to physically relax but not mentally relax?

In increasing the effect of positive feedback, you can focus an individual's attention on their muscles by suggesting that the muscles are relaxing. However, if their

> O' Mind you have forgotten your essence, and are lost in relentless speculation...you wander here and there, O Mind.
>
> Ramprasad
> (18th Century
> Bengali poet)

mind is wandering, unfocused, or distracted by anxiety-provoking thoughts and images, then how to occupy the mind becomes a major problem. F. M. Alexander (we quoted him before) was well aware of this human tendency and called it "the mind-wandering habit."

It is very simple to solve the problem by using a principle that we call **"the echo method"** which immediately increases the efficiency of relaxation and auto-suggestion a hundredfold.

## How Does It Work?

This principle is based upon the fact that we speak at an average of a 100 words per minute, but we can think four times as fast, virtually 400 words per minute. This is a very important distinction to make—that we think much faster than we can actually speak in words.

In deep relaxation we can overcome the discrepancy between thinking at 400 words per minute and only being able to speak at 100 words per minute by echoing what we hear.

You will notice during a lecture that you have had ample time to analyze, to think about, and to criticize what is said to you. You have no difficulty in keeping up with what is said and at the same time critically examining the concepts.

## How to Echo

Whenever a relaxation response or suggestion is given to you, you can verbalize, echo, or mentally repeat what you hear.

So now there are two sources of stimuli: the outside suggestion coming in to you, and your echoing it—thus making two suggestions. So you have suggestions from your own mind and suggestions from someone else's vocalization and that occupies your mind so fully that there is the opportunity to relax the mind, as well as the body.

This effective principle is virtually unknown. Simply put, the student echoes in his own mind the key words and phrases, and so overcomes the problem of the wandering mind, plus giving double reinforcement or feedback to everything that is said.

The Echo Principle is also essential with the autogenic phrases you will be taught on side two of the *Mind Magic* audio cassette. I will remind you on that side by stating "repeat mentally after me the following statements."

## Psychic Bomb

### Attitudinal Life-Enhanced Changes

A final concern is with what we might term the psychic bomb principle. Briefly, this means that positive suggestions, attempts at attitude changes, and life-enhancing psychological changes should always be dropped into the unconscious rather as when doing a "bomb run" after the resistance or flack has been eliminated. Short and general statements, rather than specific, are always better.

You will find that I have carefully selected a broad spectrum of life-enhancing attitudes at the very end of the exercise. If you should fall asleep during your relaxation session, this is perfectly acceptable. As long as possible, keep echoing or repeating the helpful attitudes that are presented to you.

If you are wondering exactly what are the contents of the attitudes that I am encouraging, then simply run side one of the tape two-thirds through toward the end and listen to the text in a fully conscious state to reassure yourself and become familiar with the suggestions.

## Contemporary Living

Lastly, I would like to remind you that **attitudes** (in the psychological and psychic world) are more important than facts. It is not the nature of the events that are so significant, but rather our attitude or the way we view the events that occur. Unfortunately, in the modern world the problem of **stress** is such that we are all suffering inordinate **distress.**

Our industrialized, highly technological contemporary society induces the fear-fight-flight response—turning on the sympathetic nervous system so that we tend in our so-called "civilization" to live in a state of "sympathocotonia," a state of ever-alert readiness against ill-sensed dangers. Modern humankind suffers chronic anxiety, rising to crescendos of acute anxiety.

Within the human mind-body complex, there is not only a fear-fight-flight response, but there is also the para-sympathetic relaxation-rest-recuperation response.

It is a sad criteria of our society that normally the parasympathetic response is never naturally educed by circumstances. Fear-fight-flight is induced nearly every day of our life, but we have to take time out and consciously learn how to bring out of ourselves the "relaxation response."

Of course, like everything in life, it is up to us; it is not something that anyone else can do for us. We have to make the time available.

**You don't find time—you make time!**

# 7

# Your Personal Stress Management Program

This program is designed for those who have accepted the adage for success: "Plan your work and work your plan!"

The success of this program is implicitly guaranteed when you organize a daily-use plan. Like everything else in life, a little patience and consistency pays large dividends.

A human being is not a piece of factory machinery that automatically shuts down at the end of the day. Sadly, we are not taught in school the principle of shutting ourselves down for a twenty-five-minute restoration period each afternoon.

It is an unbelievable characteristic of uptight Anglo-Saxon society that people are expected to work eight to twelve hours without a break (sometimes more), and then be ready for an evening of activity. The Mediterraneans have their "siesta" and even the Navy knows that a "watch" is four hours on and four hours off—but not the English or Americans!

The Mind Magic program is intended to be practiced every day—when it is, the prophylactic benefits, as well as immediate gains, are immense.

## Immediate Gains

Practiced on a daily basis, you will gain refreshment and integration of the day's activities, instant reduction of any accumulated muscular-skeletal tension, and relief of psychosomatic symptoms such as tension headache and migraines.

You may choose to alternate sides of the tape; "Fractional Relaxation" one day while lying down, followed by "Autogenic Training" the next day, sitting up.

Both sides of the tape represent the gateways to relaxation: self-hypnosis and meditation.

## Meditation Defined

At this point you should consider two very important psychophysiological definitions of meditation.

- "Meditation is **dreaming** sitting up."
- "Meditation is the moment of postponing **sleep**."

The reference to **dreaming** tells us that visions and pictures that spontaneously float through our consciousness during practice with either "Fractional Relaxation" (side one) or "Autogenic Training" (side two) indicate that we have altered our brain wave pattern into the very creative theta range—characteristic of meditation.

The "moment of postponing sleep" can be experienced with the autogenic side which is practiced sitting up. When you get so relaxed that you lose control of your neck muscles you will be having a dominant theta wave pattern in your brain. This is equivalent to "nodding off" at a very boring lecture.

The head dropping acts as an alarm monitor, preventing you from falling into non-REM or dreamless sleep. Some physiologists define non-REM sleep as "true sleep." It is precisely for this reason that Yogis meditate sitting up!

# 8

# The "Mind Over Matter" Magic of Autogenic Training

●━━━━━━━━━━━━━

## Preparing for
## Autogenic Training

Side two of the audio cassette, "Autogenic Training," is your gateway to thermal biofeedback (control of circulation in the hands and feet), voluntary control of your autonomic nervous system, and meditation. It uses the trigger word **"CALM"** as a mantra, or silently repeated trigger word, to lead you into the interior depths of yourself.

Tape the red bulb end of the thermometer enclosed in this kit to the fingerprint of the third finger (between your index and ring finger) of your dominant hand, as shown in the drawing on page 57.

The Biofeedback Thermometer is used to document the effects of stress and progress made in controlling it through self-hypnosis.

When it comes to thermal biofeedback training you should know that:

- your dominant hand is "smarter" than your non-dominant hand.

- The third finger has a more profuse blood supply and is therefore more quickly reactive (blood carries heat, and the more dilated the arterioles of your fingers are, the warmer the hands) to the autogenic suggestion statements and accompanying visualizations.

The training you are about to commence is a tremendous innovation in technique. I have amalgamated the German psychiatrist Schultz's, "Autogenic Training" (designed in 1930) with Dr. Elmer Green's Biofeedback technology.[1] Dr.

---

1 Dr. Charles Tart, *Altered States of Consciousness* (John Wiley and Sons, 1969).

Green was in charge of the "Voluntary Controls" program at the famous Menninger Institute in St. Louis, Missouri. I then integrated concepts from **Mantra Yoga** to produce a "one-stop" package suitable for introducing everyone to relaxation, meditation, and self-hypnosis.

Dr. Elmer Green work was brilliant in that he first fine-tuned thermal biofeedback with Schultz's "autogenic" phraseology which included words such as "warm" to induce relaxation.

Autogenic training was developed by Schultz as a result of the confluence of two influences upon Europe at the turn of the century; the Europeans had been reading reports of Yogis demonstrating cardiac cessation and other "autonomic nervous system gymnastics," and at the same time there was a tremendous interest in the phenomenon of hypnosis. Schultz took the self-volition of the Yogis and the rich visual imagery of hypnosis and combined them into "autogenic" or literally "self-generated" training.

In 1969, when Dr. Wolfgang Luthe reviewed the psychophysiological evidence of the benefits of autogenic training, the results equalled, and in some cases exceeded, later research on one popular, well-publicized form of meditation.

Note that the autogenic training is intended to become a **daily destressing practice** which will induce the same state as any form of meditation, and in most cases do it faster.

By making time to **destress** each afternoon we can lessen the amount of **distress** in our life.

## The Secret Trigger Word

The secret word is "calm," and I will explain the secret of the word "**CALM**." I did not invent the use of the word "**CALM**" within the context of an autogenic training program. In fact I first heard it used with autogenics by a female psychologist twenty years ago at an American conference, and to my shame I cannot even remember her name.

Three years later the full implications of the word, in terms of psychological effect (psycho-linguistics), origin (etymology), meaning (seman-tics), and its relationship to Mantra Yoga (sometimes called "Yoga of sound") became fully apparent to me.

It is intended that the word "**CALM**" will acti-vate the relaxation response in you, even in a working, open-eyed situation. It will take a num-ber of daily repetitions for this response to be elicited—exactly how many varies from individual to individual. I like to use the Indian numerological figure of 108, and say that is the maximum number of repetitions necessary.

After a certain number of training sessions, just closing your eyes and silently repeating the trigger word **"CALM"** will induce a trademark meditation state which should be maintained for twenty-five to thirty minutes each day. Daily practice with the autogenic training on side two of the cassette, and later just mentally repeating the code word **"CALM"** maximizes the benefits. This effect is straight "Pavlovian" conditioning, and is the basis of behavioral psychology.

## Sitting Up Position for Autogenic Training

Side two, "Autogenic Training," of your *Mind Magic* audio cassette, is best listened to sitting up in a comfortable chair or lounge.

The feet should be firmly supported by the floor, exerting pressure against the soles of your feet (preferably you should wear socks but not shoes). In other words, do not have your feet dangling to reach the floor—use a cushion to rest them on if necessary. A large telephone book with a towel wrapped around it makes a good foot support for students with short legs.

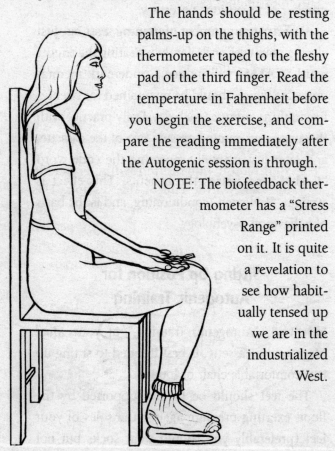

The hands should be resting palms-up on the thighs, with the thermometer taped to the fleshy pad of the third finger. Read the temperature in Fahrenheit before you begin the exercise, and compare the reading immediately after the Autogenic session is through.

NOTE: The biofeedback thermometer has a "Stress Range" printed on it. It is quite a revelation to see how habitually tensed up we are in the industrialized West.

**Seated Position for Autogenic Training. Note the hands resting on the upper legs with palms up.**

# What Can Happen with Your Hand Temperature After the Technique?

Three possibilities exist:

1. **Your temperature increases.** This happens to eighty-five percent of students in the first session. Often the lower your beginning hand temperature (80° for instance), the more dramatic the increase into the very "relaxed" range (95°+). This indicates you have locked into the technique.

2. **Your hand temperature reading is exactly the same at the end of the session.** This means a little more practice is needed to lock into the technique.

**Biofeedback Thermometer in Position.**

Employing the "Echo" principle is very important—you will need to repeat each autogenic phrase I say to you on the tape without judgment or expectation.

3. Your hand temperature is actually a few degrees lower at the end of the training session than at the beginning! This is the situation where you have tensed and "tried" to make it happen. The solution here is to focus on feeling tingling and warmth, and on visualizing the fingers turning flushed and red.

Situations 2 and 3 indicate more gentle, effortless practice is required. Thermal autogenic training is a craft, not an art, and may be mastered by anyone willing to practice. (The table below categorizes conditions by specific temperatures, in both Fahrenheit and Celsius.)

| Autogenic Temperature Ratios | | |
|---|---|---|
| Below 80° F | TENSE | Below 26° C |
| 80° – 90° F | NERVOUS | 26° to 32° C |
| 90° – 94° F | CALM | 32° to 35° C |
| 95°+ F | RELAXED | 35°+ C |

## Cool hands — Warm Neck: Your Personal Thermal Biofeedback

As well as checking your temperature with the thermometer before and after each autogenic training session, don't omit the "hand on the back of the neck" experiment we taught you earlier. See the section: "What Is Autogenic Temperature Training?"

If your thermometer reading at the outset is less than 90° Fahrenheit, then your hand will feel cold on the back of your neck, or at least cooler. Always put your hand on the back of your neck to check the temperature before and after the session.

The thermometer reading is only an intellectual notation, but many people find the increase in hand warmth, as experienced on the back of the neck (at the end of the session), is a surprise and an immediate emotional confirmation of success.

## Why Should My Hand Temperature Be Lower When I Am Stressed?

Biologists believe this is a vestigial reflex in modern man, and that the reflex's importance has diminished somewhat. Physiologists call it the principle of "Brain Sparing."

"Brain Sparing" is a basic rule that in any perceived emergency the body must spare all possible sugar and oxygen for the vital tissues of brain and heart; consequently nature reduces the blood supply (since blood transports sugar, oxygen, and heat) to the hands and feet.

In a sense we over-react to any threatening stimulus that presents itself, even below the threshold of our awareness, by taking blood out of the limbs and thus lowering temperature.

This peripheral vasoconstriction of the blood vessels feeding the feet and hands is so strong and constant that a new medical procedure has developed in the last twenty years.

When someone has fainted or appears to be in a coma, you never take their pulse at the wrist (radial artery), as invariably it will be absent—leading to the false conclusion that their heart has stopped.

You may know, or have noticed on the TV dramas (e.g., "ER") that the staff go straight for the large artery in the neck (the carotid) which feeds the brain and consequently will always be pulsing if the heart is beating.

## What Do I Need to Know About a Practice Schedule?

My friend Dr. Timothy J. Lowenstein, Ph.D., is one of the leading authorities in American Thermal Biofeedback technique and technology. In fact the Stress Thermometer you are using is designed by him and distributed by his Conscious Living Foundation at Drain, Oregon.

In regard to practice, I could not do better than quote him:

"The following four suggestions can enhance your learning to relax:

1. Initially, practice in a quiet environment, wearing loose clothing.

2. Practice an hour after eating.

3. Try to practice at about the same time each day so your body will develop a rest habit.

4. After about the tenth session, try relaxing in a more realistic, active setting.

"Do this test after every ten sessions to see how well you can rest in the midst of noise and disturbance."[2]

---

2   Lowenstein, *Conscious Living Foundation Newsletter*, 1996.

## What Is a Normal Temperature?

Again quoting Dr. Lowenstein, "What is a normal temperature? 98.6°? This is the body's average core temperature. What is a 'good' temperature? First feel what takes place inside yourself. I like to see the temperature increase a good 5° to 10°. The overall goal is an ending rest temperature of 95°. The goal is to be *a master of stress and for you to be the master of your actions and reactions rather than letting your environment dictate your response* [T.M. by Dr. Lowenstein]—*to control your own reactions rather than being controlled by events outside yourself.*"[3] [Italics mine—JM]

3  Ibid.

# 9

# The Secret of "CALM" as a "Bija Mantra"

●━━━━━━

## Defining Mantra

I define a Mantra as a "Mind Tool," derived from the Sanskrit prefix *Man* meaning "mind" (Gr. *Menos*; L. *Mens*; English *Mental*) and the Sanskrit suffix *Tra* meaning a "tool" or an "instrument" (perhaps cognate with the English word "trowel").

Another way of expressing this would be to say that a mantra is an audible or inaudible (silent) sound vibration that is used as a tool or device to alter states of consciousness (ASCs).

If you find the concept of an "inaudible sound vibration" a contradiction in terms, I would remind you of ultrasonic devices (e.g., dog whistles and the physiotherapists' ultrasound instrument) and infrasound (e.g., pre-earthquake vibrations that small animals pick up long before the actual quake), as well as the phenomenon of **sub-vocalization.**

**Sub-vocalization** is a concept that deserves a comment. Mantra yoga teaches that sound vibration has a least four levels of manifestation: audible, whispered, subvocal, and transcendental (molecular). I am expressing this with roughly equivalent English terms.

At this point you may have the horrible feeling that I am about to launch off into some abstract, abstruse discussion of Hindu metaphysics, but I won't inflict that on you!

What I am emphasising is that the **mental repetition of "CALM" has profound vibrational effects,** even at the level of subvocalization. When we "think" a sound or read "silently," our vocal cords are still vibrating. This is the reason ENT surgeons currently do not allow their patients to read after major throat surgery involving the larynx.

"Bija" means "a seed," and therefore a **Bija Mantra** is a "seed sound" that, when chanted audibly or mentally will produce inner growth and evolution—and just as the acorn seed contains the tree, so the Bija Mantra contains compressed spiritual potential.

Bija Mantras have several characteristics:

1. They are monosyllabic, e.g., Ram (the Bija for a psychic center associated with fire and the solar plexus) versus the Gayatri Mantra which consists of twenty-four syllables.

2. Each Bija Mantra consists of a single "phoneme," i.e., the smallest part of speech which differentiates one word from another by sound; e.g., "Lam" versus "Ram"; "L" and "R" represent phonemes. They are the only sounds that distinguish "Lam" from "Ram."

3. On the whole, Bija Mantras may terminate in either/or "m" or "ng."

It therefore follows that the word **"CALM"** (although an English word, it is of Latin origin, as we shall see) fulfills the criteria for a Bija Mantra. It is monosyllabic, ends in "m," and the phoneme is "C" (e.g., "Palm" and **"Calm"**; "P" and "C" are phonemes).

CALM

I will suggest to you that the mental repetition of the word **"CALM"** will exert as profound an effect as a Sanskrit Bija mantra and any of the so-called T.M. mantras (most of which are not Bija Mantras).

## The Psycholinguistic Magic of "CALM"

Warmth is associated with relaxation, melting away tension and drowsiness. When you silently think the word **"CALM"** you are evoking from the unconscious those very qualities. **"CALM"** comes from the Latin root *calor* which means "heat" as in "calorie" (a unit of heat).

In English we talk about "becalmed at sea" and "a calm sea" or a "calming influence"—all are indications of stasis, stability, and the absence of tumultuous circumstances—the very things we seek to establish within our nervous system through meditation.

### The Mysterious Magic of the "M" Labial Sound Ending "CALM"

In Sanskrit (an Indian classical language), "M" and "ng" have a special sign when they are used as an ending. This sign is called an *Anuswara* which means literally "little heaven," so called, perhaps, because the chanting of these sounds produces a "heavenly" state of mind.

In terms of psycholinguistics, the associational reverberations of the "**m**" sound ending "**CALM**" are universally powerful. Consider:

1. "mm-mm," an international sound signifying "assent, agreement, yes."

2. "mmmmmmmmmmmm" is a spontaneous, transcultural expression of pleasure and appreciation.

3. Humming is often an automatic self-soothing device when we are tense; the labial "mmmm" vibration instinctively relaxes the nervous system.

When you are asked to mentally repeat the word "**CALM**" at the end of the autogenic training, the "m" vibration is the doorway to deeper and deeper levels of meditative relaxation and freedom from stress.

The *Mind Magic* program is a complete key uniting East and West, ancient and modern.

You now possess a powerful tool in the form of your *Mind Magic Kit*.

The keys to reducing psychosomatic illness and initiating psychological change are now **in your hands**!

## Magic Melatonin Meditation: A Final Secret!

You can take advantage of the technique for using **"CALM"** as a Bija Mantra and Swami Sannyasananda's research (see appendix 2). Before bedtime quietly gaze at a candle flame for ten minutes while thinking silently the mantra **"CALM,"** then closing your eyes and continuing to go deeper inside yourself for another ten minutes with the **"CALM"** meditation.

This technique is known as *Tratak*, and Satyananda Yoga specializes in quite a few forms of this method. There are two basic rules for arranging the candle in a dark room.

The candle flame should be exactly at eye level. It should be equal to the distance from your eyes to your outstreched arm, so that your second finger (the Saturn or *Shani* finger in Indian palmistry) would just reach the flame.

There are three factors to keep in mind for the practice:

- While gazing quietly into the candle flame, fixate your gaze gently and inhibit the blink reflex as much as is comfortable.

- For the first ten minutes repeat "CALM" silently while gently contemplating the flame.

- For the next ten minutes close your eyes and contemplate the candle flame after-image that will appear in your third eye while silently repeating "CALM."

I have seen the research graphs—by the second night you will be soaking your brain with melatonin secretions.

## Mind Magic: A Positive Approach

As you commence this life-changing program and establish the **Mind Magic** routine as a daily practice, contemplate the words of the late President Franklin D. Roosevelt, featured here.

When all is said and done, we must remem-

> Men are not prisoners of fate, but only prisoners of their own minds.
>
> Franklin D. Roosevelt
> Pan American Day address
> April 15, 1939

ber that emotion can literally kill! Vesalius, the

sixteenth-century anatomist, died of shock after opening the chest of a cadaver he was dissecting to discover the heart still pulsating.

For most of us, negative emotion kills us not so spectacularly, but more insidiously through contributing to and accelerating such illnesses as high blood pressure, heart disease, diabetes, cancer, arthritis, rheumatism, asthma, and hayfever.

**Mind Magic** practices are the single most significant investment you can make to assist physical and mental health.

# Appendix 1

# The Bihar School of Yoga

Under the direction of Paramahamsa Niran-janananda Saraswati, the following facilities are available:

## International Yoga Fellowship Movement

The International Yoga Fellowship Movement (IYFM) is a charitable, philosophical organization, founded by Paramahamsa Satyananda with the aim of creating global awareness of Yogic science, practices, and lifestyle, in order to promote optimum physical health, mental well-being, and spiritual upliftment. The IYFM is an "umbrella" organization for the institutions described on the next three pages.

## Bihar School of Yoga

Bihar School of Yoga (BSY) was founded as a charitable education institution in Mugger, Bihar, in 1963. Today it is acknowledged for its high standards of teacher training, yoga courses in health and stress management, and advanced sadhana programs such as Kriya Yoga, Kundalini Yoga, Swara Yoga, and Tattwa Shuddhi. Qualified sannyasins from Bihar School of Yoga conduct lecture tours, seminars, and conventions worldwide. It is one of the first institutions to initiate and train both female and non-Indian sannyasins.

## Bihar Yoga Bharati — Institute for Advanced Studies in Yogic Sciences

Bihar Yoga Bharati (BYB) was established as a charitable education institution at Munger in 1994. It is the first institution of its kind to impart comprehensive Yogic education leading to certificate, diploma, and graduate level qualifications through the faculties of Yoga Philosophy, Yoga Psychology, and Applied Yogic Science. It offers complete academic Yogic education and training in the traditional gurukula or ashram environment. This combination of academic training and residential ashram lifestyle helps the student imbibe the yogic principles in an integral way. It ensures that, along with an intellectual yoga education, each student imbibes the spirit of seva (selfless service), samarpan (dedication), and karuna (compassion) for humankind.

## Sivananda Math

Sivananda Math (SM) is a charitable social institution founded in 1984 that is devoted to Swami Sivananda's principles of service, love, compassion, and charity. Sivananda Math is actively helping to develop the rural and deprived communities by providing shelter to the shelterless, employment to the unemployed, education to the uneducated, and medical help to the sick. Services are provided free of charge and are available to all, regardless of religion, caste or creed. In the future, Sivananda Math aims to construct model villages with wells, schools, libraries, community halls, research centers, and hospitals, to uplift the lives of those in need within the poorer sections of rural society.

## Yoga Research Foundation

Yoga Research Foundation (YRF) is a research institution founded in 1984 with the aim of providing an accurate assessment of yoga practices within a scientific framework, and to recognize yoga as a science essential for the development of humankind.

For further information regarding courses and Ashrams in your area write:

Bihar School of Yoga
Ganga Darshan
Munger Bihar 811201, India

# Appendix 2

# Swami Sannyasananda's Melatonin Research Project[1]

———●———

Greg Tooley's research project involved monitoring melatonin levels around midnight, whereas my research looks at melatonin levels around the time of onset of melatonin, which differs for each person, but occurs some time between sunset and the individual's normal bedtime. By exploring the effects of different neural inputs using certain Tantric yoga practices, we can figure out how the brain is wired up and functions as a whole. To be able to do this work a system with a stable common marker or neurological flag is used to determine what happens to that marker when we manipulate internal states. The marker for my research is the hormone melatonin.

———

1   Text of Swami Sannyasananda's report on his melatonin research, reprinted with his permission. [Edited for clarity—CH.]

Melatonin is a pineal hormone implicated in the control of a wide array of behavioral and physiological rhythms that include movement, sleep cycles, body temperature regulation, cardiovascular function, stress responses, the female estrous cycle, and many other endocrine processes. Melatonin is also a useful marker in examining many disorders of rhythms, and is an extremely important substance for a number of reasons.

The pineal gland, a small pea-sized organ deep within the brain, produces most of the melatonin in our bodies, though small amounts are produced in the eyes and also in the gut. Normally the pineal produces low levels of melatonin during the day and higher amounts at night. Exposure to light at night is followed by a drop in melatonin levels, since the eyes are functionally connected to the pineal gland by a series of neurons.

Reduction of melatonin at night by any means increases cells' vulnerability to carcinogenic agents. An increased cancer incidence has also been reported in environments exposed to higher than normal artificial electromagnetic fields that lead to a reduction in nighttime levels of melatonin. Melatonin is a potent oncostatic agent; it prevents both the initiation and promotion of cancer, and therefore plays an important role in the immune system. It is a potent antioxidant and may provide significant protection against cancer. Melatonin induces activated T cells to release opioid peptides with immune-enhancing and anti-stress properties. These peptides cross-react and bind specifically to thymus receptors, driving an immune recovery after elevated corticosteroid levels associated with immune responses and/or stressful situations.

Because of the powerful effects of melatonin, there are many research programs, often using animals, to model various effects. Human physiology is different to animals, though, and as such some of this research is of little use or relevance to humans. The practice of yoga does not require animal experiments and makes use of live human volunteers, yielding valuable information. There are two main areas of interest for me regarding melatonin research and the psychoneurophysiology of certain Tantric yoga practices. One is the practice of Nadi Shodhan Pranayama (alternate nostril breathing), and the other is the practice of Tratak (focusing the eyes by staring at a candle flame, Yantra, or dot). Both of these practices affect the brain in profound ways.

## Nadi Shodhan Pranayama

It is well known in yoga circles that breathing selectively thorough either nostril has either an activating effect or a relaxing effect on the sympathetic nervous system. Nadi Shodhan Pranayama affects the brain by alternately stimulating the right brain and then the left brain. Air flowing through the nostrils stimulates nerve endings just underneath the mucous layer inside the nostrils. As each side of the body is governed by nerves originating in the opposite side of the brain, so stimulating airflow in one nostril increases nervous activity in the brain on the opposite side to that nostril.

Each side of the brain specializes in certain activities, and the autonomic nervous system is also correspondingly stimulated and relaxed via this pranayama. Increasing the flow of air in the right nostril stimulates the sympathetic nervous system, which increased heart rate, produces more sweaty palms, dilates the pupils, and opens up the lungs—the fight or flight system. Increasing the flow of air through the left nostril, however, stimulates the parasympathetic nervous system, which increases digestion, lowers the heart rate, and relaxes us. By practicing Nadi Shodhan pranayama we are helping to balance both of these systems in relation to each other, as well as balancing brain activities.

Now the pineal gland has both sympathetic and parasympathetic nerve fibers controlling it. The practice of forced single-nostril breathing is able to change autonomic functions as well as blood glucose levels, and hormone levels in the blood are also linked with the nasal airflow cycle.

Experimental results clearly confirm that parasympathetic dominance via forced left-nostril airflow produces higher concentrations of melatonin than sympathetic activation via right-nostril dominance of airflow. This can be achieved by lying on one side, where pressure receptors along the sides of the torso shift the flow of air to the uppermost nostril. Manually obstructing the opposite nostril in a delicate manner or using a special crutch (Yoga Danda)—often used by yogis under an arm to shift the swara on demand—works equally well.

# Tratak

The Tantric practice that clearly produces the most melatonin is Tratak. It involves focusing the eyes by staring at a candle flame and also helps to balance both sides of the brain stem. Experimental evidence shows that the practice of Tratak directly stimulates the pineal gland to produce more melatonin. Secretion of melatonin is regulated by the suprachiasmatic nucleus (SCN) of the hypothalamus, which is in turn regulated by light via the eyes—hence the connection with Tratak—and the effect is cumulative. The second night's levels were always found to be higher than the first, so it seems it would pay to do a little candle gazing before bed at night for a restful sleep, to de-stress and re-arm the immune system.

These two Tantric practices are linked in their effects on the brain's production of melatonin but via completely different neuronal pathways. Forced left nostril dominance directly stimulates the pineal to make greater amounts of melatonin, while Tratak seems to work via the SCN in the hypothalamus to produce it earlier.

## Chakras

Further exploration of the medical literature strongly indicates direct neurophysiological links between certain chakras in the body, in particular **Lalana Chakra** and **Ajna Chakra**.

In Yogic circles, Lalana Chakra is an important but little-known chakra located in the soft palate behind the nasal sinus. In anatomical terms it is known as the *vomeronasal organ* or sometimes *Jacobsen's organ,* and is important in various Kundalini practices. The Lalana Chakra is thought to be a vestigial organ in humans, but it is very active in lower animals as a sensory organ that functions between taste and smell. It is an important influence in reproduction and sexual behaviors because it monitors pheromones and other sexual excretions. There is medical evidence of a functional vomeronasal organ in fetal humans and in some adults. The neuronal connections are still there though, even if the organ is not fully developed. The hypothalamus of the brain governs this organ directly, as well as automatically shifting the flow of air in the nostrils from side to side in a regular rhythm known as the "Nasal Patency Cycle."

Yogis know Ajna is very important and it is a well-known chakra used in many Kundalini and Tantric practices. It is directly related to the pineal gland, which is in turn also governed by the hypothalamus and is highly affected by light via the suprachiasmatic nucleus.

It is both interesting and very useful to be able to easily manipulate internal hormonal and physiological states. The therapeutic implications of being able to alter one's metabolism by simply changing the breathing pattern or by staring at a candle for a while are far more valuable than just a mere relaxation response or simple meditative exercise.

NOTE: Swami Sannyasananda Saraswati is currently completing research projects concerning the neurological effects of these Tantric practices at Adelaide University Medical School. He can be contacted at:

P.O. Box 101
Campbelltown, SA 5074
Australia
phone 61 8 8369 0663
or fax 61 8 8369 0840.

## Appendix 3

# Emotional Damage Control

●━━━━━━━━━━

## Instant First Aid for Negative Feelings!

My friend Swami Divyananda Saraswati is fond of quoting Sri Aurobindo's statement: "Most of our lives are lived in empty agitation."

Often that is the way we feel in our daily lives—and possibly much fuss about nothing!

Nothing has changed in 400 years—we can still become the victims of self-engendered turmoil that exhausts us. I have found it very useful to consider a particular Western therapy for directly tackling the source of self-induced agony. This system is

> My life has been full of tragedies, most of which never happened.
>
> Michel de Montaigne
> 16th Century

the Western equivalent of Gnana Yoga and Vedanta. There are exercises by which through sheer reason we can haul our misperceptions up on a leash.

I have always maintained that psychotherapy is Western Yoga and what I am about to share with you I do not ask you to agree with, but please experiment with this material. You will feel more positive, walk taller, and maintain focus and direction by trying these principles.

The place to start is by realizing we often have false ideas concerning ourselves and our expectations about life. These concepts or premises about living, if accepted as true, create emotional havoc in daily life.

The psychologists say "we progenerate our psychopathologies," meaning that the neurotic or incorrect attitudes that we adopt are learned as children, from our parents, teachers, and the cultural influences under which we live. The real horror is that we, in turn, often teach these emotionally destructive ideas to our children.

Another way of expressing this is that unless we are careful we may merely exist in the shadow of our parents.

American psychologist Dr. Albert Ellis developed a now well-established school of therapeutic intervention, called "Cognitive Therapy" or "Rational Emotive Psychology," in which common fallacies are identified and rigorously challenged. You may want to read his classic *A New Guide to Rational Living* (Wilshire Book Company, USA).

Albert Ellis, Ph.D., is the Executive Director of the Institute for Rational-Emotive Therapy in New York. He has authored or edited over fifty books including *Sex without Guilt; Reason and Emotion in Psychotherapy;* and *How to Stubbornly Refuse to Make Yourself Miserable about Anything, Yes Anything!*

A wonderful internal freedom can result when we recognize and consciously reject these false premises and in so doing begin to enjoy a life devoid of self-torture and endless recriminations.

I have permission from the Wilshire Book Company to quote Ellis' "Fallacies" and I have selected nine of them for your consideration. Ask yourself how many of the following mentally unhealthy premises you have accepted in your life. The commentary underneath each quote is mine.

## Fallacy Number One

**"I must be adequate, achieving, and competent in all possible ways if I am to consider myself a worthwhile person."**

Philosophically, it is imperative that we learn to live with and accept our personal failings. No objective standard exists by which you may decide you are a "success." Success is determined by whatever you believe it is for you personally.

Ask yourself if you are merely subsisting on the unfulfilled dreams of your parents. Swami Divyananda says that a child is just a canvas upon which parents "splatter paint."

If your idea of success is running a corner store and you achieve this, then you are as big a success as a millionaire business tycoon. Managing a household efficiently or fulfilling a desire to write a book make you a success if these are your goals.

True success is being able to live your life in the way you find satisfying—not anyone else's way, but *your way!*

Our society promotes contradictory ideals such as "a successful young executive is a ruthless competitor, a modest winner, and a good loser." Careful thought reveals that the above statement asks individuals to contain within the framework of their personality mutually exclusive traits. Don't be fooled by such garbage.

The best key to achievement is to discover how you may release the innate creativity, which is possessed by everyone. Creativity lends itself to satisfaction in all areas, from baking a cake to repairing a car.

## Fallacy Number Two

**"I should be dependent on other people, and it is necessary to find someone stronger than myself whom I can lean on."**

Be careful, women particularly, about believing this idea. One can rely on nothing but the self. No state, nation, political system, religious dogma, marriage partner, relative, or friend can be completely relied on.

Change is a fundamental law of life, and the only really worthwhile dependence is on the self. The object of all true philosophical systems is to lead the student from a state of dependence to one of independence. When we have crossed the river of life, why still cling to the raft?

Relaxation, autogenic training, and meditation can allow you to build a pillar of strength within yourself and perform the alchemical transformation from being "alone" into being "all one."

By the same token we must accept that humans are naturally gregarious, and being independent should not exclude interdependence, promoting satisfactory support systems at work and home.

One of my old lecturers defined mental health as "the ability to work and love." Both these activities involve interaction with others.

## Fallacy Number Three

**"As an adult it is necessary that I be liked and appreciated by nearly every important person in my society."**

The human condition is such as to encourage feelings of insecurity and anxiety. The more insecure we are, the more reassurance we crave from others. Face the truth that you cannot be loved or liked by everyone. Someone will always dislike you (perhaps with good reason!).

The only approval that really counts is self-approval. Have you come to terms with yourself? If you essentially dislike yourself, why should others like you? It is a great secret that only those with self-approval dare to risk giving credit to others.

A closely allied fallacy is: "Some members of society are wicked, bad, villainous, and it is absolutely necessary that they be blamed and severely punished for their way of life."

What do you think about alcoholics, prostitutes, criminals, homosexuals, divorcees, adulterous marriage partners, and abortionists? "Who will cast the first stone?"

If you accept that some people are intrinsically evil (rather than unhappy, brain-damaged, or else free of superficial moralism), be careful you don't end up stoning yourself to death at a crisis period in your life.

If you base your life on the fallacy of judging others, guilt will create a living hell for you if you commit adultery, have an abortion, become divorced, or experience homosexual attraction.

Perhaps it is worth contemplating that the bulk of serious criminal activity, drug addiction, and alcoholism are the end results of genetics, personality disturbances, and neurological damage—all often compounded by terrible childhood abuse.

In the sphere of human emotions and sexual activity, be cautious about moral judgment of others, for one day you may discover yourself in the very situation you have condemned.

## Fallacy Number Four

**"It is an absolute tragedy and a personal catastrophe when things are not the way I very much wish they were."**

Remember the old saying that bars do not a prison make? The prison is created by mental attitudes, not situations or the environment.

Do not be tricked into thinking human happiness is externally caused and that you possess little or no ability to control your sorrows and tensions. Although our problems in life cannot always be eradicated, our attitudes about problems can be changed.

> We are all born in the gutter but some of us are looking at the stars.
>
> Oscar Wilde

The difference between a tragedy that emotionally cripples one individual and a similar tragedy that another person adequately continues to cope with life in spite of is simply a difference in mental outlook, mindset, or attitude. Avoid converting problems into worries.

You may feel I am being very trite and superficial in suggesting this—the reality perspective is that the majority of occurrences in our life that upset us most definitely are not CATASTROPH-IC—tragedy is a word we should reserve for major national calamities or events that reach into the heart of many across international boundaries, such as the recent sad death of a princess.

## Fallacy Number Five

**"If something is dangerous or potentially dangerous, I must be terribly concerned about it and should constantly dwell on the possibility of it occurring."**

A major key to philosophical equilibrium is living in the present. There is a distinct line drawn between awareness of possible danger in certain situations versus a fearful concern of phobic proportions in which the mind is living in imaginary anticipation of future calamity. When we become anxious over an imagined future calamity

> Our worst misfortunes never happen, and most miseries lie in anticipation.
>
> H. de Balzac
> (1799–1850)

we are really reacting to the fantasy of an event that has just occurred in our mind as if it had occurred in reality.

We know that a natural ebb and flow in the affairs of humankind exists. We can learn how to use the potential inherent in each segment of time as it arises; however the concept of cycles must never be misconstrued as an encouragement for neurotic concern with the future or fearful antici-pation of natural testing phases which represent an inevitable part of living.

## Fallacy Number Six

**"It is easier for me to avoid rather than face certain life problems and responsibilities."**

Problems are best coped with by going through rather than around them. Why? It is simply a mat-ter of psychic economy—our mental energy must be used wisely and repressing or suppressing problems, i.e., trying to ignore them or push them out of conscious awareness, uses up more psychic energy than facing them ever does.

If I submerge a ping-pong ball (a problem) underwater (out of sight), the minute I release the ball it pops up to the surface (conscious awareness).

The only way I can keep the ball deeply immersed is by constantly holding it down with one hand. This means I have crippled myself, losing the use of one arm, which is devoted entirely to holding the ball under.

Do you cripple yourself emotionally trying to hold down problems? Don't avoid problems—face them! If you need help and encouragement go to a close friend and if necessary don't hesitate to get professional support.

## Fallacy Number Seven

**"My past history is a crushing determiner of my present happiness, and because something once strongly affected me it must continue to similarly affect me."**

When a past event influences your present behavior, your mind is divided against itself. Brooding over the past wastes energy, as does day-dreaming of the future.

Know that all human enterprise is often accompanied, unfortunately, by an inordinate desire to succeed (living in the future) and an inordinate fear of failure (based on past experience of failure).

You can actually train yourself to focus your attention on the now, thus helping to release

> Worry never robs tomorrow of its sorrows, it only saps today of its strength.
> A. M. Cronin

the grip of the past. Refusing to count chickens before they are hatched is good mental hygiene and is the basis of Karma Yoga. Now is the time.

## Fallacy Number Eight

**"There is always a right, correct, and perfect solution to human problems and it is a major catastrophe if this perfect solution is not worked out."**

All problems may be faced, but not all can be solved—some situations are so messy and intricate that they can only be accepted or endured. Avoid flagellating yourself if you fail to find the answer to your marital difficulties or misunderstandings in relationships and business.

Each person's feelings are in a constant state of flux and what was once harmonious understanding may tomorrow become unharmonious misunderstanding. Remember that there seldom is a real right or wrong—there are just people with conflicting feelings.

Human relationships tend to be built upon a flimsy spider web. Often we like people for no better reason than that they appear to like us. When you fully understand how true this is you will cease searching for "perfect" solutions.

It is an illusion that we like or dislike people—
what we like or dislike are the feelings that contact with them induces in us.

**Fallacy Number Nine**

**"I should become extremely upset over the
problems and disturbances of other people."**

Sympathy, contrary to popular belief, is not the
most efficient way to help others with their problems. Sympathy involves identifying yourself with
another's emotional state, and then two unhappy
people exist instead of one.

Empathy, not sympathy, is what is required.
Empathy is understanding another person's feelings and, above all, accepting them. Do not turn
their problems into your problems.

Any attempt to give advice or sympathy is
based on the false notion that people cannot solve
their own difficulties. Each person contains the
solution to alleviating his own stress, given an
accepting listener, as surely as the egg contains a
yolk. Because others are disturbed do not fall into
the trap of feeling you also must be upset.

In India they would call "comfort" an aspect of
Bhakti Yoga. An extension of this concept is
becoming involved in the problems of the world

> Physicians should remember that although they can rarely cure, they can usually relieve and they can always comfort.
>
> Sir William Osler

and community at large by reading daily newspapers, watching the news on television every night and listening to the news on the radio throughout the day.

This may seem a little fanatical, but I strongly suggest that if you are constantly depressed and anxious about the state of the world, try ignoring the media—you may be amazed at how your tension level drops!

Believe me—anything you really need to know someone will always tell you! Psychologists are now becoming aware of how we live in an age of information overload—absorbing the news daily is a form of mental poisoning more potent than any current ecological disasters, and the equivalent of taking a bath in sewage.

I selected these nine of Albert Ellis' fallacies to kick-start you on a re-evaluation of your personal attitudes and beliefs. I am very fond of Indian Numerology so I tend to round everything off in groups of nine.

I can suggest what others and myself have found helpful to do with these concepts:

### Exercise One
Read over all nine of the fallacies every night before going to bed and select one to think about as you are falling asleep. However, this is not a good idea if you are going to get upset over a particular fallacy and experience insomnia.

### Exercise Two
Write one fallacy in your personal diary every day and contemplate it throughout the day. See if you can catch yourself indulging in that particular false belief during the day.

### Exercise Three
Every time you realize you are reacting emotionally based on one of the fallacies, rationalize it out of your head by reading the part of this chapter dealing with it and actually state to yourself, "**I don't have to go on acting as if this attitude or belief is important and true.**"

## Exercise Four

Photocopy this appendix, cut out each fallacy with my commentary, and carry a different one with you each day to take out of your purse or wallet and study at odd moments.

## Exercise Five

Cut out particular fallacies you need to work on and tape them up in a prominent place—on your bedroom or bathroom mirror, or even the kitchen cupboard. This will remind you to think about and reject the fallacy.

## Exercise Six

This is a graduation technique to really become familiar with the nine fallacies (for those that like the Kabala, you can consider there are ten—"a closely associated fallacy" could make the tenth).

You can play a psychological version of pick-up sticks, solitaire, or, in company, by carefully photocopying the chapter and cutting up the pages in such a way that Ellis' Fallacies (the ones in quotes) are separated from my commentaries.

You then shuffle the eighteen or twenty pieces of paper up in a large mixing bowl and pluck one piece of paper out.

If you pluck out a fallacy, write a commentary to it based on your personal experience. If you pluck out a commentary, write about or discuss the fallacy associated with it.

Taking these exercises seriously will improve the caliber of your psychological life significantly. I have seen several hundred patients benefit from these concepts and I have personally found them very helpful.

When these **Principles of Rational Thinking** are applied we can solve the conundrum:

**Are we in the prison
or is the prison in us?**

# Daily Monitoring Chart

Daily Monitoring Charts are a common tool in clinical psychology and are quite useful if you can discipline yourself to actually fill them in. Using the chart on pages 102–103 for just two or three weeks will give you amazing insight and control.

Note that the "Feelings Before" and the "Feelings After" sections are divided into nine sections on an imaginary scale. "5" is in bold type, and represents a relatively neutral state—neither particularly "tense" nor particularly "relaxed." (You may want to make photocopies of the spread of two pages on one sheet of paper for convenience.)

You will have to examine your feelings and decide what is neutral for you. It will help if you write down several words to describe what the worst scale of "1" is for you and what the best scale on the calm or "relaxed" "9" end is.

Many of my patients and students find it very beneficial to begin using this chart by alternating between side 1 (Fractional Relaxation) one day and side 2 (Autogenics) the next day.

Be aware that even if your temperature is in the "relaxed" scale of 95 F° you will still get immense benefit from doing the autogenic training daily or every other day.

Use the "comments" section to make a note about the major factor in that day that you perceive as contributing to your happiness or unhappiness. After two weeks you may discover a pattern that is quite revealing.

I suggest you cultivate the habit of engaging in and actively seeking an activity every day that you enjoy and that therefore constitutes a daily reward!

# Daily Monitoring Chart

Beginning the Exercise

| Day | Date | Starting Temperature | Feelings Before<br>Tense          Relaxed |
|-----|------|----------------------|-------------------------------------------|
| Monday | | | 1 2 3 4 5 6 7 8 9 |
| Tuesday | | | 1 2 3 4 5 6 7 8 9 |
| Wednesday | | | 1 2 3 4 5 6 7 8 9 |
| Thursday | | | 1 2 3 4 5 6 7 8 9 |
| Friday | | | 1 2 3 4 5 6 7 8 9 |
| Saturday | | | 1 2 3 4 5 6 7 8 9 |
| Sunday | | | 1 2 3 4 5 6 7 8 9 |
| Monday | | | 1 2 3 4 5 6 7 8 9 |
| Tuesday | | | 1 2 3 4 5 6 7 8 9 |
| Wednesday | | | 1 2 3 4 5 6 7 8 9 |
| Thursday | | | 1 2 3 4 5 6 7 8 9 |
| Friday | | | 1 2 3 4 5 6 7 8 9 |
| Saturday | | | 1 2 3 4 5 6 7 8 9 |
| Sunday | | | 1 2 3 4 5 6 7 8 9 |
| Monday | | | 1 2 3 4 5 6 7 8 9 |
| Tuesday | | | 1 2 3 4 5 6 7 8 9 |
| Wednesday | | | 1 2 3 4 5 6 7 8 9 |
| Thursday | | | 1 2 3 4 5 6 7 8 9 |
| Friday | | | 1 2 3 4 5 6 7 8 9 |
| Saturday | | | 1 2 3 4 5 6 7 8 9 |
| Sunday | | | 1 2 3 4 5 6 7 8 9 |

# Daily Monitoring Chart

## Ending the Exercise

| Ending Temperature | Feelings After<br>Tense          Relaxed | Comments |
|---|---|---|
| | 1 2 3 4 5 6 7 8 9 | |
| | 1 2 3 4 5 6 7 8 9 | |
| | 1 2 3 4 5 6 7 8 9 | |
| | 1 2 3 4 5 6 7 8 9 | |
| | 1 2 3 4 5 6 7 8 9 | |
| | 1 2 3 4 5 6 7 8 9 | |
| | 1 2 3 4 5 6 7 8 9 | |
| | 1 2 3 4 5 6 7 8 9 | |
| | 1 2 3 4 5 6 7 8 9 | |
| | 1 2 3 4 5 6 7 8 9 | |
| | 1 2 3 4 5 6 7 8 9 | |
| | 1 2 3 4 5 6 7 8 9 | |
| | 1 2 3 4 5 6 7 8 9 | |
| | 1 2 3 4 5 6 7 8 9 | |
| | 1 2 3 4 5 6 7 8 9 | |
| | 1 2 3 4 5 6 7 8 9 | |
| | 1 2 3 4 5 6 7 8 9 | |
| | 1 2 3 4 5 6 7 8 9 | |
| | 1 2 3 4 5 6 7 8 9 | |
| | 1 2 3 4 5 6 7 8 9 | |

# Bibliography

Benson, Herbert, and Miriam Z. Klipper. *Relaxation Response*. New York: Avon, 1976.

Dreaver, Dr. Jim. *The Ultimate Cure*. St. Paul: Llewellyn Publications, 1996.

Ellis, Dr. Albert, and Robert A. Harper. *A New Guide to Rational Living*. New York: Wilshire, 19??.

Lowenstein, Dr. Tim. *Conscious Living Foundation Newsletter*, 1996.

Tart, Dr. Charles. *Altered States of Consciousness*. John Wiley and Sons, 1969.

# Index

# ☽ LOOK FOR THE CRESCENT MOON

*Llewellyn publishes hundreds of books on your favorite subjects! To get these exciting books, including the ones on the following pages, check your local bookstore or order them directly from Llewellyn.*

## ORDER BY PHONE
- Call toll-free within the U.S. and Canada, 1-800-THE MOON
- In Minnesota, call (612) 291-1970
- We accept VISA, MasterCard, and American Express

## ORDER BY MAIL
- Send the full price of your order (MN residents add 7% sales tax) in U.S. funds, plus postage & handling to:

  **Llewellyn Worldwide**
  **P.O. Box 64383, Dept. (K–475–8)**
  **St. Paul, MN 55164–0383, U.S.A.**

## POSTAGE & HANDLING
(For the U.S., Canada, and Mexico)
- $4.00 for orders $15.00 and under
- $5.00 for orders over $15.00
- No charge for orders over $100.00

We ship UPS in the continental United States. We ship standard mail to P.O. boxes. Orders shipped to Alaska, Hawaii, The Virgin Islands, and Puerto Rico are sent first-class mail. Orders shipped to Canada and Mexico are sent surface mail.

**International orders:** Airmail—add freight equal to price of each book to the total price of order, plus $5.00 for each non-book item (audio tapes, etc.).

**Surface mail**—Add $1.00 per item.

## DISCOUNTS
We offer a 20% discount to group leaders or agents. You must order a minimum of 5 copies of the same book to get our special quantity

## FREE CATALOG
Get a free copy of our color catalog, *New Worlds of Mind and Spirit*. Subscribe for just $10.00 in the United States and Canada ($30.00 overseas, airmail). Many bookstores carry *New Worlds*—ask for it!

**Visit our website at www.llewellyn.com for more information.**

Psycho-Spiritual
Techniques for
Health, Rejuvenation,
Psychic Powers &
Spiritual Realization

Dr. Jonn Mumford
(Swami Anandakapila Saraswati)

# A CHAKRA & KUNDALINI WORKBOOK
## Psycho-Spiritual Techniques for Health, Rejuvenation, Psychic Powers and Spiritual Realization

**Dr. Jonn Mumford, OD, DC**
**(Swami Anandakapila Saraswati)**

Spend just a few minutes each day on the remarkable psycho-physiological techniques in this book and you will quickly build a solid experience of drugless inner relaxation that will lead towards better health, a longer life, and greater control over your personal destiny. Furthermore, you will lay a firm foundation for the subsequent chapters leading to the attainment of super-normal powers (i.e., photographic memory, self-anesthesia and mental calculations), an enriched Inner Life, and ultimate transcendence. Learn techniques to use for burn-out, mild to moderate depression, insomnia, general anxiety and panic attacks, and reduction of mild to moderate hypertension. Experience sex for consciousness expansion, ESP development, and positive thinking. The text is supplemented with tables and illustrations to bridge the distance from information to personal understanding. In addition, the author has added a simple outline of a 12-week practice schedule referenced directly back to the first nine chapters.

*A Chakra & Kundalini Workbook* is one of the clearest, most approachable books on Yoga there is. Tailored for the Western mind, this is a practical system of personal training suited for anyone in today's active and complex world.

**1-56718-473-1, 296 pp., 7 x 10, 8 color plates, softcover   $17.95**

# ECSTASY THROUGH TANTRA

### Dr. Jonn Mumford, OD, DC

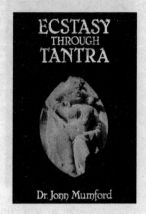

Dr. Jonn Mumford makes the occult dimension of the sexual dynamic accessible to everyone. One need not go up to the mountaintop to commune with Divinity: its temple is the body, its sacrament the communion between lovers. *Ecstasy Through Tantra* traces the ancient practices of sex magick through the Egyptian, Greek and Hebrew forms, where the sexual act is viewed as symbolic of the highest union, to the highest expression of Western sex magick.

Dr. Mumford guides the reader through mental and physical exercises aimed at developing psychosexual power; he details the various sexual practices and positions that facilitate "psychic short-circuiting" and the arousal of Kundalini, the Goddess of Life within the body. He shows the fundamental unity of Tantra with Western Wicca, and he plumbs the depths of Western sex magick, showing how its techniques culminate in spiritual illumination. Includes 14 full-color photographs.

**0-87542-494-5, 190 pp., 6 x 9,**
**14 color plates, softcover**                                        **$16.00**

## MAGICAL TATTWA CARDS
### A Complete System of Self-Development

### Dr. Jonn Mumford, OD, DC
### (Swami Anandakapila Saraswati)

Tattwas—the ancient Hindu symbols of the five elements (earth, air, fire, water and ether)—act as triggers to the psychic layers of our mind through the combined power of their geometrical shapes and their vibrating primal colors. Tattwas are amazingly potent "psychic elevators" that can lift you to ever higher levels of mental functioning. The Hermetic Order of the Golden Dawn has used the tattwas for meditation, scrying, astral travel and talismans. Now, with this new kit, you can use the tattwas yourself for divination and for bringing yourself into altered states of consciousness.

The twenty-five tattwa symbols are printed on 4" x 4" cards in flashing colors (colors that when placed next to each other appear to flash or strobe). Although the geometrical shapes of the tattwas have long been an integral part of the Western Magical Tradition, the flashing colors and their divinatory aspects have never before been available as the complete integral system presented here.

**1-56718-472-3, boxed set: 26 full-color cards and 5³⁄₁₆ x 8, 288-pp. illustrated book**                     **$29.95**

## CHAKRA THERAPY
## For Personal Growth & Healing

### Keith Sherwood

Understand yourself, know how your body and mind function and learn how to overcome negative programming so that you can become a free, healthy, self-fulfilled human being.

This book fills in the missing pieces of the human anatomy system left out by orthodox psychological models. It serves as a superb workbook. Within its pages are exercises and techniques designed to increase your level of energy, to transmute unhealthy frequencies of energy into healthy ones, to bring you back into balance and harmony with your self, your loved ones and the multidimensional world you live in. Finally, it will help bring you back into union with the universal field of energy and consciousness.

*Chakra Therapy* will teach you how to heal yourself by healing your energy system because it is actually energy in its myriad forms that determines a person's physical health, emotional health, mental health and level of consciousness.

**0-87542-721-9, 256 pp., 5¼ x 8, illus., softcover**　　　　**$9.95**

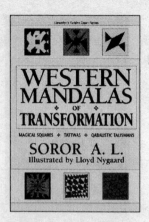

## WESTERN MANDALAS OF TRANSFORMATION
### Magical Squares • Tattwas • Qabalistic Talismans

**Soror A.L.**
**Illustrated by Lloyd Nygaard**

More than any other book, *Western Mandalas of Transformation* reveals the uses of astrological and Qabalistic talismans for your spiritual use. Now you can learn the mysteries hidden in the ancient system of magical squares—some of which have never been published in the Western Magical Tradition! Geared toward both the beginner and experienced Qabalist, step-by-step instructions teach you the process for creating your own mandala-talismans. Discover how to use a mandala to acquire a magical Guardian Angel and the correct guidelines for obtaining spiritual guides. Learn the traditional magical seals of the Golden Dawn and the powerful Tattwa system.

This complete guide contains special sections on the meaning of numbers, planetary attributes, and sound and color healing. You get explanations of the secret techniques for awakening these images in your subconscious to energize your chakra system and personal aura. There is also a section on gematria for the seasoned Qabalist, and a full chapter on Daath and Pluto. Instruction in *Western Mandalas of Transformation* clears up mistakes and "blinds" in many other talismanic books of this century and is accompanied by more than 150 illustrations.

1-56718-170-8, 272 pp., 7 x 10, color plates, softcover   $17.95